Natural Sustenance

Poems
Selected from
the
Chapbooks

by
Nick Fleck

*One impulse from a vernal wood
May teach you more of man,
Of moral evil and of good,
Than all the sages can.*

-William Wordsworth

Published by Human Error Publishing
Paul Richmond
www.humanerrorpublishing.com
paul@humanerrorpublishing.com

Copyright © 2014
by Nick Fleck
All Rights Reserved

ISBN: 9780983334491

Natural Sustenance

Front Cover:
collage by Margot W. Fleck (www.margotwfleck.com)

Back Cover by:
photograph was in the public domain.

Illustrations by
Margot W. Fleck

Human Error Publishing asks that no part of this publication be reproduced or transmitted in any form or by any means electronic or mechanical, including photocopy, recording or information storage or retrieval system without permission in writing from Nick Fleck or Huma Error Publishing .

For Margot, Robyn, and Mike,
with my love and respect.

Natural Sustenance
Table of Contents

Two War Poems 6
The Earle Sonnets 7
Walter Sam Riley 15

Voices 19
Sparrow Hawk 20
The Red Maple 21
Untitled 22
Black Nebula 23
Blueberries 24
Milkweed 25
Fisherman 26
The View from Mt. Grace 28
Untitled 29
Thursday to Thursday 30
After Calling Verizon 31
July 3, 2013 32
Yesterday 33
Sleepwalkers Along the Connecticut 34
A Sage 35
Mood Indigo 36
Transformation 40
Dewey Avenue 41
Transformations 43
The Littleton Diner 45
In Morning Fog 47
Winter in March 47
Voices 48
Cormorants 50
"You're a Poem" 51
Inevitability 52
In the Retirement Home 53
Stages 54
The Open Door Frame 55

Untitled	57
Adam's Farm	58
Untitled	59
For the Demaines	60
On a Photograph by Markowitz	61
Untitled	62
A Call	62
for M.S.	63
Uncle Charlie	64
Stratton Mountain, June 9th	65
Stratton Mountain, October 9th	66
One Wild and Precious Life	67
Mt. Moosilauke, N.H.	68
Geese	69
A Brown Creeper and the Snake	70
Late November	72
Edward Hopper	73
For my Senior who had a Stroke	74
Four Gifts	75
A Mountain Hike	77
Lily Keep	78
A Crossing	79
The Bangor & Aroostook R.R.	80
Red-Bellied Cooter	81
Mt. Grace	83
Seasonal	84
The Sparrow Hawk, Revisited	86

-from **The Kinsman Poems**	87
Arrival	88
Dawn Under the Kinsman Ridge	89
Mountain Air	90
Plums	91
Under the Mountain	92
Mt. Kinsman, Dusk	92
Easton, N.H.	93
Reflection	93

Acknowledgements	94

Two War Poems

The Earle Sonnets

1.
How would you describe his oblong face?
It is not possible for it is so long and drawn
with a nose fit for some stone age race,
a strong sense of smell, and a look of brawn.

A broad brow and ears too large like portabella
and his eyes a coyote's: joyous, serious, knowing;
yes, as serious and sound as an ape's—a fella
in a cage with iron bars and concrete flooring.

He could mend any rusted, frozen marine engine
to make it hum like a Singer so that the ship's
nose would gently, definitely rise on the tide's rips.
They say it was the war that turned him to gin;

They say combat set him to sit unemployed
at the wharf's edge, to accept a life destroyed.

2.
What can a man do altered by the Pacific campaign?
Return home with fame where his wife, his son—
born after his enlistment—and daughter wait in vain?
What can a man do for a family struggling

At the hem of the village in a tar-paper shack?
What can he do? His nightmares repeat a startling—
Japanese Guernica or a flash as bright as
the first flash of dawn's early light. A mechanic

as fine as any the military trained: that he was.
At night, waiting for his release, he cries.
The military Doctor stamps his papers: "sane."
He has nowhere to go, but home. Look at his eyes.

They live in the realm of torn and separated ties:
His wife, his son, his daughter; at home he lies.

3.
There was a boy; there was a man, too.
He was a man, now a boatman invisible;
The other a boy, fourteen—one of the innocent few.
Both know the transformation of this fable.

Days off they spent with pistons, oil pans,
carburetors, plugs, and gaskets—to break down
and rebuild a '36 Gray Marine engine:
the joy of grease, dirt, bolts, and nuts; this fun

accompanied by tales of world war two, of Japs
and illicit sale of cigarettes: cash for his wife,
the unknown son, and teen daughter; of collapse
and an internment in a white-washed ward; of strife

and of a release. To be sent home cured—a shadow
of the first class seaman-mechanic he was.
Now with seasonal employment ferrying cargo
for the sons of the priviliged; that's what he does:

Forced to fish and poach—to sink so low;
To struggle. He was a man; he becomes the boy's woe.

4.
He is lazy, a man whose spirit
the Pacific theatre battered
while he jury-rigged the shattered
LSTs and launches that spit

into the crossfire and the mined surf
his shipmates, buddies like blind boys
sent by fathers to face a field's turf.
None told how recovery too destroys.

He's a self's shell; he sits alone
jigging a line and bobber
on the town's wharf like a robber,
seeking without seeking: to atone.

He is in the eyes of the saved
An empty role, a knave enslaved.

5
Does he have a name? he holds no job
for longer than a season. He's not disabled,
he earned an honorable discharge. It's fabled
He was the USN's number one mechanic: no slob.

Does he have a name? he's the town's number one
bum—a chance for charity; they divert
their attention when he kills, skins, hides in dirt
a doe not in season; he does it not for fun.

Does he have a name? is he someone known?
or is he like the fauna and flora?
a genus, a species: Homo poora?
Distinguished and defined no better than a crone.

Does he have a name: yes, there's a rumor
that he is someone: he's Earle Maria Bloomer.

6
He's no older than the Camp's teenage potwasher
yet so ancient that his face is a field
of twisting alleys from spring's runoff; he's wiser
than the Elders in the village who yield

not to responsibility's tempting call.
During the morning slack he and the boy
sit and talk: never cry; with laughter enjoy
this intermission: he tells not of his country's fall.

The town fathers, pleased with the boy's ingenuity,
praise the man-like teen and for the man
they pass the ammunition; they are no fan
of this Vet who receives for his service no gratuity.

Cured and diagnosed recovered and sane
he was discharged marked like Cain.

7.
He eats lunch in the kitchen with Gus,
a French Canadian caretaker for the Camp.
At times they are joined by laconic Russ
a part-time grounds keeper. The stamp

of their ways appeared in impossible schemes
solved: the illiterate Gus built without a drawn plan
a chest of drawers from an upright piano; to redeem
himself, Earle tuned a motor to an efficiency utilitarian;

and a two-story, framed house built by Gus in
a Canadian winter with Earle's hand.
Both undesirables cast in sin:
Saturday nights for games, dances, and firebrand.

One drowned himself in the lake he navigated;
One froze on the porch he built; both desecrated.

8.
Earle lasted the summer   that was enough
        from there   he again   went without a job
never applied for unemployment   if a mob
had formed   they would have tarred and feathered the stuff
he'd become   which syndrome   shell-shocked
was he too smart   like old man coyote   for a role
of a boyman in war   his wife saw   his mind locked
his eyes held   the retreat of fear   his soul
like a slow boat swamped   sunk   into a deep rift
she tries to resuscitate him   she sits and cries
with him   he wanders   sits on a bench adrift
no tears left   no fears surface in his flat eyes
did he have a name   was he someone known
will his heritage be sown   do boys have fame

9.
What can an innocent boy mean for such a man,
a survivor of drownings in the Pacific, the runner
of contraband—alcohol and tobacco. What plan
had this Vet to honor a friend or a dead gunner?

What can be made of this invention of a man
corrupted by courage and death in the Pacific theatre?
How can we know the dark nights among a clan
formed by our guardian children, mere amateurs

in the fine points of killing. Did he wish for the young
not to be in the undying company of the unconscious
practitioners of war? What made him casually tongue
these tales of heroic horror, to spin stories fractious

to the beings of the teller and the disciple of fate?
as if this were to explain his disciplined hate.

10.
What loss would drive a forsaken boy to seek
in summer's innocence the love of a man,
an emptied shell of a former self? to speak
and to listen in trust to such an artisan?

Evenings after the campers and boats were bedded,
After the pots and pans stacked, the floor swabbed,
after the last sound of taps faded, they quickly headed
for the infirmary's solarium where the sleep-robbed,

lonely boy and this sleepless survivalist of battles
and slaughters went to play canasta or charades.
With the camp's nurse they talked without masquerades:
they were friends and equals in life's chimerical prattles.

Was it escape from agony or the nurse's feminine charm
each sought at day's end, to save them from night's dark alarm?

11.
Everything goes. An oriole lies under a window
her neck broken; nothing comes around. Near
dawn Earle left, in tears kissed his soon to be widow.
It was time: no longer would gin or tales

address or abate the image of a buddy's stare:
smarts, smells return stormier than Pacific gales.
He knew it must appear an accident, a moment
when the working mind relaxed, lapsed not from despair.

He took his lunch pail: a Snickers Bar, a coolant,
two peanut butter & jam sandwiches, and an orange
to his temporary employment: a quick repair
of the Kineo launch. The losses he will avenge.

He'd never learned to swim, thus this end of an affair
with crafts, with war, with tales to make boys aware.

12. In Memoriam

Earle Roger Maria Bloomer. I found his stone
Along side villagers in the cemetery abutting the CP
Railroad. The grass was mown, the flowers grown
longingly in plastic pots, flags for veterans, and algae

engraved on the granite and marble memorials:
Rows of families, of neighbors, of friends, and of heroes
made by accidents and by wars. I'd read the editorials:
"Brave seaman and mechanic served and left a widow

lessened by an untimely death at present undetermined."
Of relatives and his post-service time little mentioned.
On his gravestone: Found Peace Sought, 1956, age 33 years.
May we readers and recorders discern more from the fears

etched upon the feminine faces of men more gentle than
regulations approve, men as sensible as was this Midshipman.

Walter Sam Riley: a Monologue at Sunrise

I am old, my son, as you can see. With legs
unbalanced I, on my third leg, walk.
Last evening my daughter led me along
an old tote road through mud and alders,
over moss-slicked logs, and a winding path
ingrown with fir and spruce. Such is the way
to this northern woods camp and its tract.
Without my Jack Daniels the pain would have
crippled my effort; without my half pint
I would have fell along the way. They, the others,
laugh at my morning, intestinal need
for prune juice strengthened with whiskey.
And now we talk in the dawn while they
still recline in slumber wasting another
chance to see the sun rise. [He struggled,
teetered to stand and turn to face the sun,
raised his arms as in an embrace, and spoke.]
Sun, again we have made a full circle.
I and you are old friends thankful for
another day. [He returned to the old rushed
arm chair and sat quietly.] You know each
of us—the sun, you, and me—are sojourners.
    My wife, a doctorate in cellular botany,
taught me that everything is an experiment.
And that these have neither successes
nor failures—there is no such meaning
for all experiments come to their end.
The sun and I are beings that run our course.
Chance rules: there's no sense, no nonsense.
    Do you have tea? I have black tea
for breakfast with Jack Daniels, if you
don't mind. Do I talk too much; just say
yackety, yack, yack, if I repeat myself.
That's what my grandson does: 'Yackety,
yack, Grandpa.' I gave up coffee on the four
o'clock watch when my only companions
were the stars; that's when I came to know
the skies. I still see the stars and constellations,

but my memory fades as the stars fade
under the approach of a storm; and so
I forget their names; I used to know them all.
You don't mind do you my cigar? Yes,
one morning Cookie brought me a cup
of the coffee pot dregs, all gummy like the mud
I walked in yesterday; and I heaved
and heaved over the leeward gunwale. Four
in the morning and sick on a rolling sea.
That was the last of coffee for me.
You don't mind if I pour a little more
Jack Daniels into my tea? My arthritis,
you know. I could use a touch of hot water, too.

* * * *

   What are we? I have friends who say
intelligent life exists only here, on Earth,
we are the one, the quintessence of nature.
How could it so be in such an immense Universe?
They ask me which church I attend. I attend
none. We are sojourners formed by chance,
not by a god. They can believe, but I quickly
learned that this is a world of infinite
variation, the joy of random rhythms.
I am a forester by training. The key
is to know that we are such small
mutable bits of matter that exist
as we are for a brief term. Imagine
all those suns and planets and no other
life. Yes, you and I are experiments!
I like to tease those believers: I tell them
I am here as a memory bank for
the scientists on Alpha Centuri.
I gather into my sponge-like brain
all that my senses perceive. They will come
for me and bring me to their civilization
to extract and examine my memories.
Then they will know about the planet, Earth.
They will see what a species we are:

wars, hatred, the rich and the starving.
And they will note the unchecked population
growth of our kind. My wife explained
about species populations: the rise and
the fall of numbers. I think that humans
are nearing the apogee of population.
Then like lemmings falling off a steep cliff
into the ocean, billions will die. It is a
natural career. We are part of nature.

* * * *

My father became sick and died after
the World War from mustard gas. I only
remember him in his lingering sickness.
My mother, a Bell Telephone operator
found only occasional corporate employment
during the depression. We learned to survive.
When she had work I spent the winter with her;
the others she sent me to my grandmother.
With Pearl Harbor I knew I had to join
the navy. The sea was in my blood.

* * * *

I am now pleased to return
to northern Maine, to the woods and to
the gleam of beauty found in this quiet
area remote from the noise of civilization.
No cellular phones, TV. Not even a radio.
Sorry, forgive me, for I come to tears
as I tell you this; it is my way of life. My wife,
who suddenly died three years ago, said:
there is no meaning, no progress, no purpose.
That is nature's way. She was a scientist,
a humanist. I too studied Biology.
A high school biology teacher excited me
with life. Thus I became a forester.
I spent one summer as a fire watch
on a mountain in Idaho. The next

I worked at the base camp as a cook
and dispatcher for the new watchers.
We are all watchers and dispatchers. And
a third summer I spent in Patten, Maine, at
the edge of a wilderness like this, and
employed in a plywood factory.

* * * *

We've had a good talk.
And you an English Teacher. My one failure.
It is rare to find someone who knows, appreciates
the view that all life from the smallest elements
to the largest gathering of dancing particles
is nothing more than elemental chance.
We have understood each other. Get me
some more hot water. I get two cups out of
one tea bag. Thanks.
           I am Walter Sam Riley.
My friends know me as Walter, my family
calls me Sam.
    Listen, the others come for breakfast;
we will be silent. I will go split
some fire wood. The double bladed axe
replaces my cane. I must do my small part
in this camp, for the joy, the peace held
in these woods, by this lake.
                    For I am
Walter Sam Riley, Forester again.

Voices

Sparrow Hawk

He is a watcher of our ways;
not of our interstellar routes
but of our current maze.

Superior to our swirlings
he is an observer of our days:
our comings, and our goings.
He finds a perch whereon he reigns
and if he alights on neither crag
nor post, the falcon hovers on wings,
in an incessant zigzag,
motionless in air, where he surveys
the grassy shoulders in summer haze.

When I hold my palm against the sun's rays
to shade my vision, I see him
suspended, silhouetted. I succumb
to summer heat and have a whim
that he observes me whirl
on singing tires just as he notes
the locust singing a welcome
to the noontime heat. He furls
his wings and plunges:

my loneliness reappears,
rises with the grasshopper
or the vole spiked on his spears.

He rests upon a cable; a knight.
And I, I rush on beneath his sight.

The Red Maple

Silver ridges on silver bark
branch into a silver candelabrum
spread against infinite blue
where each sun-traced sliver
terminates in a red plume.

I lie naked on my back
and listen to the solo
of the Purple Finch
lost in the myriad of scarlet tips.

I want to sketch the Red Maple in bloom:

With a silver-tipped quill
and a wash of water color
I'd brush sprays across ink
on depthless blue paper
as the Maple brushes my spirit
through her scarlet tips.

The billowed cumulus
stationed behind her fingertips
draws my focus:

the Maple spins,
the Earth spins,
I spin;
and the notes of the scarlet-capped Field Sparrow
accompany spring's
regenesis.

Untitled
-In my beginning is my end

At night she hears
as in a dream
the silent whisper
the final words spoken
to her inner, awakened ear
and she descends
the slippered stair
into the den,
a makeshift room with a blend
of a desk, a bed, and a stuffed chair.
It is the voice she knows,
the last breath
speaking from the intense
moment of silence
and calm that attends a death.

Yes, at night she hears
and bends her steps,
as darkness nears,
to where her mother rests
as ever, and the Word
like the world is borne
on the death we mourn.

-for Mary Kennedy

Black Nebula

1.

At dawn
I've been fishing,
tricking feathers across
the shadowy surface,
casting for the morning rise
when dreams like trout
leap into the air.
How many escape unseen?
Many I have cast for and missed.

I read to aid my sleep.
Beside the bed rests a pen and notebook for my dreams.
I record one
and let others slip from my sleepiness.
The last to escape
slid back into the pool's depth
with my fly hooked in his lower lip.

Will the rusting hook fester
to curse him with pain?
will starvation set in?
or will panic rise in a frenzy of feeding:
leaping through the surface,
dancing at dawn, day, and dusk?
I see him disappear
his sooty back bending
under the surface in the overcast sky.

I pass from the reservoir's edge
knowing that the god of trout
waits for me, fouled.

The Blueberries

The blueberries
in July sun   ripen
     a boy   nearly naked
with an olive glow, baked
sits among the bushes
and stains his palms
as he feeds;

beside him
his black and white
Siberian Husky
(so gentle with children)
rests on her haunches and chews
the berries before she swallows each:

two gods they rest side-by-side

In a motion—
as swift as a tree swallow's feeding dive
upon calm waters—
she slit the throat of an Olive-back Thrush.

Milkweed

In the borders of our field
a family of milkweed
stand together ... a great
gathering ... talking.

In a delicate wind
you can see their words
stray, little parachutes.
A tongue not open

to translation though
understood, clear
in their drift for us,
who watch the October

sun slip behind the
rainbows of
seasonal leaves:
so like us; so like us.

Fisherman

1.
Up the river
A fisherman casts
His artificial lure
Toward the sandbar's ripples

And if by design
Or chance he brings
Into his boat a catch
He quickly detaches

His success and drops
It into the shallow depths;
What is it for this man's
Ego that drives him thus?

He floats by standing near the bow of his boat.

2.
It matters not that it ends when it ends
The day is clear
The sun high
The robin cocks her head and sings

in the exultation
of now

3.
Why does he in the heat
Of summer's sun cast
His hope into the darkened depths?

There is a pleasant breeze
Found under the solitary maple
In the mowed & pleasant lea.

There is a place beside his friends
On a checkered picnic robe
Where wine is sipped and bread's broken.

Yet he persists to stand half naked
In the burning noon
And drift upon the river's soft tide.

The View from Grace   -Mid-October, 2012

A Turkey Vulture flutters
      perhaps the last to leave
like a Monarch
on raised wing tips
silently passing across the golden ridge
of birch and popple.
      After she has slipped
gracefully over and down behind the north slope
I am still
with her—I can see
the wobbles of her secure flight, adjustments
in thermals and the light breezes,
winds from the North.
      Little moves
        a rustle—perhaps a vole
or Northern Pine Squirrel;
A slight movement:
        —on a naked maple's lowest branch
        a Gray-cheeked Thrush,
        returning from the taiga, rests—
no one else …
      I sit on a path facing south
centered in the Sun's warmth—
      with peanut butter and blackberry jam
on my home-made oatmeal/molasses bread
kneaded in a 1901 Universal Bread Maker—
      like one my Mother turned
      and hers before her.
      Turning the handle swirls the dough
into a ball—turning, turning
as the Earth turns
as the departed Vulture turns
as the migrant Thrush turns and
as you
            and I turn …

Untitled

The old roads,
whose ways are filed
and hidden in saplings of maple and hemlock,
exist on the old county maps ...
they are the ways of deer and cat
as their indented double tracks bend in the underbrush
to pass through a watercourse
or a break in a stone wall where once a pasture stood,
where cows or sheep grazed ...
these are the paths of the unconscious
that wander through shadows
where new growth disguises a gone day ...
as these parched maps
describe the cellar holes and wells of transient
substance ... so the faintest ways are stored
in archival marrow ...

Thursday to Thursday
    (thursday, november 16, 1978*
    thursday, november 23, 1978)

thursdays are beau
utiful for in no
vember we celebrate
our love for foe
with fasts and feasts
with fatted beasts
in memory of our dear fate
received from those now deceased;
thus in our land we subjugate
those we starve and violate:
the in-di-an at winter's gate
brought grace & our due we ate....

on reservations we now keep
in kindness them and so we reap
thursdays fast
for our consciences to expiate
and thursdays feast
for us a slaughtered beast.

---

*The first International Fast Day

After Calling Verizon
-for Thoreau

Henry, after his mid-afternoon saunter,
Dropped in today for tea
And found no one at home, but
A nearly deaf robot, named Achilles.

A fire simmered on the brick hearth;
A whippet stretched on the double niche Kazak
And Achilles sat warming in a cat-scratched
wing back chair caped in a wool frock.

Henry spoke again to the robot. Achilles
without inflection said: "I do not
understand you. Say Yes or NO."
Henry yelled in an eloquent counterplot:

"May I sit before your fire? —""I do not
understand you. Say Yes or NO."
He tried again: "May I have some tea?"
He wanted to tell him about a meadow

and the arrowhead he chanced upon. His profile
staid—with silence and an expressionless smile.

July 3, 2013

Early evening
the light slight upon
two wandering Grackles
adorned in purple-hooded cassocks:

one follows an avenue paved
one zigzags across my maple-shaded lawn ...

In the sun
atop a tall, slender flower stem
that bends like a blade of grass
translucent blue wings
of a darning needle ... crystals ...

we rest dazzled
in the liveliness of late sun —
enlightened ...

Yesterday

I came to a clearing.
The trail — an old tote road —
I rambled without bearing.
The way unhallowed

passed through birch,
through beech and oak
where once farm folk
were neither poor nor rich.

The woods a skin of snow
and sunlit.
The straight lines of trees
cast long shadows — a doe

stood frozen still,
her tailed swished,
she turned and bounded
to vanish behind a stand of young hemlocks.

The best of chance and will
is in these woods grounded.

Sleepwalkers along the Connecticut

Far under the bridge span
        a pair of beavers begin
their life's work to dam
        this wide expanse of current.

Someone should stop and yell:
        "you cannot find the river's
depth or breadth." But they simply fell
        birch, cherry, and popple

along the east shore where
        the flood plain supports
such growth from spring's fair
        season of sun and floods.

Above, I stand fifty feet or more
        from where they in an unconscious
pattern start along the shore
        to construct a home to store
for winter, for children fodder copious.

But who understands what beavers
        know? who can truly speak
of life's spring rains and fevers?
        who knows what they will seek?
who of us are the true perceivers?

A Sage

I see an old man sitting
on the front door stone
where he is quiet, alone
in the sun's setting.

He rises thrice or more
at night; his cancer no
longer in remission or so
he feels. What is it for,

these years without sense:
the sun continues with a chuckle,
a Blue Jay nests in the honeysuckle,
and a catbird mews on the fence.

He raises his arm, his fist
and shakes it as if he knows
who sent these blows.
There is in his eyes a mist.

The tests lie for they say
there's no "detectable trace",
that he lives in fate's good grace
in these waning hours of his day.

Or is it a long lingering past
of unease, of an acidic tone
that's the remnant of what's known
from the shadow he cast?

On the stone is an old man
sitting alone in his age.
I know him as a sage,
this lost talisman;
this once passionate seer
now caged by an ancient fear.

Mood Indigo

this room
hung
with turkamen carpets is my cave.

one day when my friend comes and knocks on my glass door
he will see me here stretched most likely in a cramped style on the
Shiraz beside the low mahogany table and white rocker with the music
stand spilled;
no call to 911
will bring me
again to my feet.

what a romantic
notion
that scene
of Mr. Death's

His second self, Mr. Death,
will call
and my friend will try 911
the neighbors will not hear the tenor of the siren
among the many artificial vehicle warnings
and Mr. Death
will depart with resuscitation
too—no mercy

the sky—in these cold days—
passes from blue to green: three PM

But my friend
didn't arrive
didn't
send a message

so I settle into my rocker with a cup of green tea and honey

in the market
the rhythms are not jazz jamming
only words
formed improvisationally and carelessly

"if it were a rattlesnake
you'd be..."
someone a salesperson speaks of health soaps.
                                                                 her custom choice
                                                                 a feminine bar labeled
                                                                 Baudelaire

the checkout clerk counters: "have a fantastic Friday."

the worst:
   on the interstate two hours without a light: no stars, no houses, nothing only the single continuous hum behind the headlights of the last van in Maine without the big dipper or the heavenly triangle to locate the sleeping occupants of the aging van, soundless

nothing like the third floor room:
        where long beams of lights slide back and forth, back and
forth   across the walls and ceiling of my being
        these shadows of traffic on Montgomery Avenue, Haverford
        a football field and the team wooden benches before the
green   wooden stands separate my grandmother's attic
room

        —where, to relax my consciousness,
        I slept or lay awake—

from the avenue
with lights and
shadows
passing at midnight

                * * * *

who clanged in the kitchen
—the sun now up—

in the morning
breakfast in the kitchen with the black cook
kinder and gentler
than my
grandmother
eating alone in the table-clothed dining room

thus consciousness
returned:
with light
sorrow and
solitude

the day resumes yesterday

the toll gate halted us
the dark
the dream:
the two hours of unmarred emptiness

soon the others will
begin
to stir

the painless
joyless
hours of black erased

thorough and fair
in the abyss
       of not-being
we left the road at
       the toll gate,
       on the map exit ten
       the next to last exit
       before Styx

I showed him the balanced rock secure beside a little known cave
   like a room hung with rugs obscured
by the wood's second growth:
grape vines   hemlocks   saplings   &   timber trash

safe
from the trampings
of
out-of-state orange
vests

Two AM
now to dream
to enjoy
a notion of death
crystallizing suddenly
like the glass thin skim on a pail of water

Transformation

-The generative ontological process through which all things arise and pass away. David Hinton on "Tao."

The finest sculpture I made
was in autumn
when the lake was low.

The abstract designs arose
with the natural curves of the water-smooth dri-ki.

Where I found them
—in the rocks now revealed along the shore—
I took them
and stood them
            at angles
determined by the cracks in the rocks
and their own shapes,
curves clasped and braced together
at this time
of low water.

Winter will come,
snows will melt,
the lake will again rise,
and the dri-ki sculptures
will be undone.

None will come
and see
these designs of natural abstraction.

And you say, "it is a loss."

As with all things we too come
designed by footholds and shapes
to pass with the seasons' ebb and flow.

Dewey Avenue: The Berkshire Wooden Boat Company
                    -Pittsfield, Massachusetts, Noon, 11/02/01

My truck died.
He lay in the boat yard
Without pride
Across from the Victory Temple
Of the Church of God in Christ.

Not a pretty site:
Cinder blocks and paint-peeling triple deckers
Holding lives of earned spite
With weathered back porches
Near the Church of God in Christ.

Along the street
A woman dressed in sloppy orange slouches
While keeping this feat:
Ashes suspended from a white smoking tube
passing before the Church of God in Christ.

What could I do?
Wait for Triple A, listening to a scolding squirrel
Silhouetted against the clear blue
In the skeletal maple left on the Avenue
Or visit the Church of God in Christ?

In a silver
Mercedes SUV, one teen male
Under a slow setting sliver of a moon
Cruised this paved river of unseen poor
Back and forth before the Church of God in Christ.

On one spruce in a yard alone
A hand penned sign warns "No Trespassing,"
An illiterate terrier digs for a bone
Not recognizing these words of ill
Next to the Church of God in Christ.

A warning on the street:
In diamond shaped yellow, "Watch Children."
A marvelous feat
Where there are none; no skateboards, tears, or laughs
Along the avenue of the Church of God in Christ.

A man in ragged clothes
Curbed his secondhand Kia sedan
For all love the poor preacher
Entering the unlatched door
Of the Church of God in Christ.

Time has not moved
Here where the boats' remains wait resurrection,
Where lives once grooved; where
A vagrant, scruffy mutt barks at the door
Of the Church of God in Christ.

What more can be said
While sitting in the cab of a white Toyota pickup
In this yard of the dead:
Wooden hulls and ribbed skeletons
Clearly not blessed by the Victory Temple
Of the Church of God in Christ?

Transformations

1. Alone

Here I am again
knowing,
knowing which way to follow
but follow none.

I go by a bog,
along an esker ...   through pines
and poplars,
untrammeled.

And the foot asks, where now?
and the mind—alert
                    to sounds, to sights—
withers..

2. Anima Accompanied

The mountain path I trail
is a water course
of miniature dams, autumnal leaves,
cataracts, twists,
and micro-pools,   apparent
diminutive things ...

though, as for that, not
for the Pine Vole that drinks
at its edge.

3. As One

It is a boulder ...
where I sit at the bog's edge
facing the setting solstice sun.
At my feet the sphagnum:
blueberries, the red tint of heaths:

Labrador Tea, Sweet Gale, Bog Rosemary,
Leatherleaf, and Rhodora; adorned
with the tufts of the wool-bearing Cotton Grass,
rusty Tamaracks once homes to flycatchers.

I sit. I watch the fading
tints of evening
secure in Wildness.

4. Cycles

The water returns
into itself ... after passing
through the Andromeda Nebula
... along the Milky Way ...

I find three poems ...stashed
in the leaves of Mountain Poems,
Hsieh Ling-yün ...

Now at peace
I can
 sleep
from late dusk to
the light before dawn:

my occurrence appearing of itself.

The Littleton Diner

I didn't recognize the music.
It belched like greasy home fries
from the kitchen, a mixture of country, with scraps
of rap and a scratchy voice. The steady beat
was all, the rest not even ornamentation.
The beat: a mixing machine for pancakes
or eggs? I couldn't tell. I had not had my coffee.
Six AM.

Little inside had resumed.
Papers were stacked like 'homemade' pancakes
with no sweetness to dulcify
the headlines:
Car Bombing Mars Market;
Forest Fires Unite;   Two Dead on I-93
The same as tomorrow's or yesterday's.
The articles composed like these lives.
A line of blue-shirted bachelors filed
in, straddled the counter stools.
Their talk: the trading of a 16-gauge shot gun
for a single bolt deer rifle; a bargain bought:
a discarded race car with 235/220 HP engine,
with an automatic race transmission: no reverse.
One manager with his own mug sagged over his stool,
a humpty-dumpty sort with a balding, shining head:
"there's money, there's
money to be made, out there.
But the young guys today
just
want to collect their checks."

He spoke again to the sole somber server
attired in the diner's habit,
"You're awful silent today."
"I have lots to do," is her businessman's avoidance.
He's snubbed.
He doesn't care, she's a waitress.
He's the crew chief and can't be late.
As he goes so he mutters,
"There's good money to made"

and leaves a quarter for a tip.
The booths like pews nearly full.
The counter scattered with used coffee mugs.
The dish machine steams.
I still do not recognize
the choir
in the kitchen
singing the same song with another melody,
the same basso continuo.
The bachelors file out for their pickups.
The sun has risen.

In Morning Fog [Northfield, Massachusetts, 2/28/07]

A crow calls. One snowbird searches seeds
in snow where a white moss covers all
flat surfaces. — Again he calls

in an alien language of spondees,
dactyls, and anapests like a brazen trumpet.
I, too, have wanted to be a poet,

not a brook telling tales, fallacies, and fables;
not a spider constructing spheres.
The lone crow has gone; the other stays near.

The snow continues in calm air to descend lazily,
directly. The tracks in the yard fade, arranged
as tales told by words smudged.

These illusions   views   matter most of all:
visions that inscribe in the mind a wild call.

Winter in March

The long plains of white numb my spirit.
The feeder emptied; the red fox
streaks across frozen overcast, a comet
in furry black socks.

And the winds reside at home.
The voices of spring silenced
The whole plain dome
of heaven held in grey abeyance:

squirrels curl in the orchard;
doves like small rocks are perched.
My desires, my hopes torched;
aquifers through sandy soils leached.

Voices

1.
When I walk alone along trails hardly worn
I find a rhythm in my voice full of silence borne.

2. The Trail Maker
I have seen him at a distance,
Have known his orange ribbons, his markings
And his cuttings; for he is as obsessed
With his woods as the beaver is with his.

He seems to be in many places,
Leaving his white and blue blazes—
I suppose—saved for another day; but
For himself he marks and clears;
He's not a follower of others' fears.

Perchance you have seen him,
Been where he has been; seen
His round midriff and dwarf-
Likeness; have heard his axe's
Beat or the hum
Of his hand held saw.

Those of us who do not cut
But walk the trails are less
A part of where we stood.
We seem trespassers in his woods
Along the streams and shores
Of flowages: intruders among
The wild and uncomplicated
Companions of an hour's, a day's,
Or even a season's wild sphere.

3. The Bushwacker
Abhors a trail: a walk without pucker brush,
Without soaked feet,
Or a loss of location

Is a walk without vocation.
Try to follow him; see in Autumn
Where the leaves are turned,
Find a split branch
Or a boot print in the mud or sphagnum.

Where is he going?
He's not sure for it's a time of whim;
What is he doing?
Nothing; it's a saunter he seeks,

Not where a trail follows
Or ends; it is for a chance
Meeting with the omnipresent Chickadee
Or the shy tawny cast Veery.

This is the source of his appraisal:
A casual climb through Witch-Hazel
Or a sloshing through a swamp
Leaving, he hopes, no palpable trail.

4.
When ever I walk the Northfield hills
I hear the voices of women
Speaking,
Never shouting; never singing.
Unlike the kinglets'
Staccato trills they are dolce, subtle,
And just below the clarity of words.

It lifts my step
Brings a liveliness that the brook
With its whispers and minor falls
Falls short of...

Voices.

Cormorants

They sit on the deck-like chalet porch high
In the hills. Guests expected. The Woodbury
Mountains mark the horizon. Beyond, there
is the faint blue of a higher range. They sit
in silence. They have spent nearly every
subject over the last forty years. He listens
for the sound of an engine under a load
climbing toward their winding drive. Silence.
He knows that they will all be jolly,
share gin and cheese, tell some old, some
new tales; nothing halts the inevitable
movement of their frugal lives. Suddenly
he sees against the faint orange sky
of late afternoon a large V of cormorants.
Unlike migrating geese they move south silently.

"You're a Poem"

My neighbor walked her robed whippet
As I was bringing in the wood;
She saw me struggling with it
On a makeshift sled. I stood

To catch the greeting she tossed
Across the crunch of sled against
The gloom gray crust that cost
Such a trial in a field unfenced.

I was not sure what she spoke,
But I knew what she had sensed
And answered while my load of oak
Rested. In lateness the light condensed

Slowly, assuredly into a drift of dark.
They left. And I went in with fired delight.

Inevitability
-for Spud Fleck, Age 93

Is it thus imagined or is it fact?
        that we, each of us, lives
in abject solitude. I have seen
        the tracks of a coyote across
the morning field of ice & snow:
        a single track clearly headed
somewhere in the crepuscular light
        before dawn: his way not quite
straight where it wavers like
        the flame from a candle nearly spent.

Is this the path we, each of us, take
        across the fields of imagination
through the maze of our illusion?
        Do I or you know any more
than that coyote supposed he knew?
        Where are our friends? and his?
Are the slight deviations from the line
        of his travel a lapse or a distraction
angered by hunger and an unsuccessful hunt?

I stand by his tracks in the faint,
gold glow just before dawn
to ponder: do we go directly
or wander by our hungers drawn.

In the Retirement Home

-a cruel old age will soon overtake you.

This room, barely larger than my dining room
table, is where I am in the last of my resting;
it's all that's left. I sit upon my bed—hour
upon hour, day upon day, week upon week,

month upon month—in time stacked like my best
china unused, saved year upon year for guests
in my glass cabinet. I am told that my house
has sold. "Yes," I say. "It is my knitting I want."

I hear that the belongings, my belongings
have been separated, parted as I too departed.
I sit in this resting place that's fresh white.
I am as nearly naked as the day I was born

in a white Lying Inn. Now I sit here, here
where there's room for one bed, a glass table,
and a stuffed chair. I have a T.V., videos,
a few birds seen on the white snow outside

the window, and the skimpy reminder of my
past in the framed photographs of family:
a few memories skimmed from nine decades.
Here there are no ghosts to hold me, company.
It is at the last so pure, so empty …

Stages
-In memory of Spud Fleck

Beyond the walled cemetery
on route 31, there is a man,
with junked steam shovels,
gigantic rollers, and skyscraper
tall cranes, who constructs
shapes from his dreams.
On my way to lay a poem
at my mother's grave,
I stopped in his sand pit,
his stage for forms.
As I stood in wonder, I heard
another say to his Love:
"he must have been aroused,
caressed by his dreams.
Will they rust or become
another's dream
when he is gone?"
     2.
Tears...
I kneel by my mother's stone
to lay near her,
my poem.
     3.

It was a life lost:
an actress captured by convention:
The Tree Witch,
The Hill Wife,
to favor kitchens, suburban stone
gardens, and girl scouts.
Pain subdued aches
like old legs at night
disturbing the soul's slumber.
May she now lie
in comfort:
a life lost is lost forever.

The Open Door Frame

               -for C— S—

1.

If you leave your simple door frame unattended
And move like a skater on clear black ice
Across your back yard, by the popples and birch
You planted, by the tracks of cats and Gray Fox
Carved delicately in the dew damp grass
Like an artist's line, by the hermaphroditic
Scarecrow, by the neighbors sitting with coffee
And pastries while reading the requisite Times,
By the grave of The Evangelist, and if you cross
The river into what for you is as unknown
And barren as a wind-shifting desert; then
You will open abandoned lands within your
Most intimate past, an intimacy nearer
Than the open door frame you left today.

2.

The skater on black ice sees through this skin
With a clarity not offered by a glass darkly.
She leaves etchings that connect the locations
Where she knelt to observe fresh-water muscles,
Sticklebacks, and Square-tail Trout; never
Does she catch her own fair reflection so
Unlike a sick suitor looking upon a calm pool's
Surface. There is little danger of a great love
Inviting her to abandon senses and leap in
To embrace some sensual, dark, nubile
Lover. Her grace is in contained curiosity,
In a desire to observe, to wonder how such
Lives breathe; or how the figure-eights
And the circles she's carved create her world.

3.

The mirror lies. We see in it as in a glass
Darkly. The reflections are far less false,
Less definite than the images we imagine.
The tremulous Aspen to itself is
Nothing—yet its rustles soothe us as
Does a Buddhist chant. I have placed four poles
In my yard; like an incantation, from
Every angle they offer a distinct and unique
Shape. A Gray Fox threads tracks through this bamboo
Stalking our grey cat. This crepuscular hour
Hinders my view, not theirs. Does fear or hunger
Arrange this conjunction? What invisible attraction
Occurs in a room across a crowd of listeners?
Is it not unlike the Gray Fox and grey cat?

4.

Darkly.... These thoughts in a lecture hall near
A forest of birch, spruce, maple, and fir that
Has reclaimed its heritage to provide cover
For a settling of vireos, Olive-backed Thrush,
And carpenter ants—sustenance for the Pileated,
For the spirit of wildness. At its edge
Lupines, Meadow Rue, Black-eyed Susans,
And a multitude of grasses sate my desire
For an unkempt margin. Closer to my
Consciousness, my seat; I mow for sureness:
A landscape painter assures me that each
Of us does what he must to hold at bay
The predator of darkness, the fear, the wild
That lies and waits outside the simple door frame.

Untitled

After the end of a certain season
a wild comfort settles upon the lake
upon our rustic camp.

In the evening a Fisher
hunting along the shore crosses the pier
where I sit cross-legged;

she is undisturbed by my breath.

The fork-tailed swallows
skim the the calm face of the dusky lake drinking
feeding on invisible insects.

A few lazy and scarlet tinted clouds
float overhead and I am reminded of how
evening is a prelude to morning

when again I'll be
beside still waters with arms raised greeting
the sun rise.

Adam's Farm

When I drive by dairy farms
with their fields lined by white plastic parts
of a snow man not stacked —
rolls of compressed hay wrapped
too large
for any man to lift,
it is of loss, I think.

It is of summer days when chaff and sweat
mingled in torturous rashes;
it is of loading rectangular, twined cubes
up on to the faded green '36 Ford's flat bed,
of standing to throw
these hundred pound bricks into the upper loft
above the line of stanchions (the milchers now in pasture).
I wonder what country boys
do in summer
while tractors roll and lift these giant's spheres.

They never learn from the red burn of summer sun,
of the red itch of sweat and hay stalks; and
of companions
sitting with kitchen jars of water raised
from the farm's dug well, of peanut butter
and jam sandwiches wrapped in wax paper, of
the sun-dried, like the rivulets in baked fields,
farmer who knew
when to chaff us on our foolishness, our broken bails.

And I wonder about mechanism, summer
communion, and Rude Wisdom.

And empty hay lofts ...

Untitled

Just after dawn my neighbor
is out pounding wooden stakes
into the corners
of his dreams, his imagined
space: an enlarged kitchen,
a sunroom, or
a fully-equipped carpenter shop

Our unoccupied minds choose
—while lying in bed before dawn—
between activity and despair.

Layers of protection are laid down
like sand, silt, rocks
to form an alluvial fan
at the river's mouth.

Storms with their off-spring surf
invade, erode these layers.

Soon the mind—willing or not—
will seek the depths of the sea.

For the Demaines

The geese are gone today
The cornfield lies vacant
The river in the dawn's mist calm
The day's fair
The news:
Matty, at nineteen, dead.

The school bus comes; the school bus goes.
Little rests on the voices of the year.
Lunch is served; students laugh
And cry in the turmoil
Of spring's flood, now upon the plain—
A sump drowned with mountain minerals.

The earth turns; noon will come
As surely as the summer;
And soon the scarlet sun
Will set in the west; the gods demand
Too much pain of the undamned,
Of loss—the suddenness of an end.

On a Photograph by E.G. Markowitz

Upon the ghostly images of dead spruce
the morning mists
hang like Old Man's Beard lichens …
Moose are placid
where they feed on bladderwort and water shield …
Swallows erratically slap the flowage's
calm surface …

There is serene movement here
where no man fishes
though the shrill laughter of Alcyon
echoes off the hilly backdrop …
the sun has not risen; the moon has set.

Where I sit cross-legged at the water's rim
I am distracted by the faint ghostly shadows,
my ghostly self, and
what little we know of mirrored worlds.

I arise, silently with moccasined feet,
turn, and climb—in the emerging light—
to cross onto a hardwood ridge
before too much sun will wrinkle and evaporate
these arresting ghosts of dawn.

Untitled

When out walking
late in the day
and the mind is empty
with little to say;

I follow the lane
of a broken wall
through the second growth
of leaf-emptied fall,

'til I come and rest
where three walls crossed,
to sit and consider
lives passed and lost.

A Call

Where I put out seeds for the birds,
One morning, like an unspoken prayer,
A Black-capped Chickadee landed
On my outstretched hand where

In my cupped palm lay sunflowers & millet.
In the distance—so faintly, but clear
I heard beyond the rush of freight
the cries of migration   *there, there*!

You too can hear it if you stay so calm
A chickadee or a titmouse will bless your palm.

-for **M.S.**

The boy ran randomly; the dark curly haired
Girl stood still at the easel with her brush
Held high in her hand like a wand. Her arm bared
Before the imagined orchestra—the moment a hush;

She raised higher her arm then the down beat; she
In her captive pose could not see him
And his attentive prayer, his silent plea;
His fantastic admiration for this seraphim.

These two in separate imagined creations:
She preparing to paint watercolor screens
Seen inward to become her manifestations
Of nature that represent her inner dark scenes;

And he? He in his later years would recall
Her dark eyes and the terror of her suicidal fall.

Uncle Charlie

Poor Uncle Charlie
Buried today
Among the snow,
The rain, and hay.

Poor Uncle Charlie
Lived so long:
To an age
Of ripe old hay.

Poor Uncle Charlie
Buried today
After so many years
Of sunny days.

Poor Uncle Charlie's
Last five years
Of happiness in
Senility and peace,
Peace for him—
But what about us?

Poor Uncle Charlie
Buried today
Among the snow,
The rain, and hay.

Stratton Mountain, June 9th

Climbing to the peak of Stratton
in early June
is a rise back through the season:

from the Canada Mayflower,
Choke Cherry Blossoms,
and the Blackburnian Warbler

to the May blooms:
Dwarf Ginseng, Adder's Tongue
and the Clintonia's Golden flowers.

*   *   *   *

This hike, this ascension
back into spring takes my son & me
into the wild space

where time and space
are suspended into a wild place
of an eternal present:

the civilized replaced
by the sounds of Earth
intoning its incessant birth.

*   *   *   *

Our descending into summer
to civilized illusions
where the unison of my son

of me lingers from the summit:
where we heard a Wood Pewee
and now an Eastern Phoebe.

Stratton Mountain, October 9th

The beech still mind their leaves;
in plashes of rusty orange
they grace the hardwood hills.

High on the slope
the berries of The American Mountain Ash
garnish with globes scarlet.
◊ ◊ ◊ ◊
Overcast today ... nearly
No one abroad ...
not a vole, chipmunk, or mole.

An immature robin
and one pair
of Red-Breasted Nuthatches ...

My son and I step lively
against the chill
keeping warm by talk.

The frost line passed: a
demarcation of beauty where
flurries on cheeks delight.
◊ ◊ ◊ ◊
There is a certain unclear
sadness in our descent
to levels warmer

than the grey-green taiga
of the mountain's top ...
for we had not been

recently here and know
not when again we will ...
for winter's at our sill.

One Wild and Precious Life

I sit in my hospital window.
Below there is a piece of road.
It must be an unusual road
Even with its fog and solid
Center lines. The pine and the birch
Dominate my view; they obscure
Parts of the paved way: I perceive
There are three little pieces.

Cars come and cars go accompanied
By a struggling hunched jogger; a bus—
Advanced Parking on its side;
A relaxed walker, and a squat red
Fire-hydrant; No UPS or postal truck;
Never a line, as in traffic,
Of cars; steadily they alone appear,
Pass, and vanish. The road is as it is:

It comes from nowhere; it goes nowhere.
The cars appear, disappear. The jogger
Vanishes behind pines. The Advanced Parking
Van never stops, never parks, but
Comes again. Another younger, springier
Jogger passes slowly. Suddenly
A long stretch of a high cloudiness approaches
From the western horizon: I sit; I watch.

Mt. Moosilauke, N.H., 1998

With November half unborn
My son & I hiked a snow delineated
Gorge Brook Trail. The footworn
Way made our walking unintimidated.

In two weeks my radical retropubic
Prostatectomy's scheduled;
We neared the tree line's Orphic
Opening, the storm-ruled

Approach to the granite summit,
Where blizzard whirls of shifting snows
Sowed blindness, a certain plummet
Toward fears' shadows.

Only the white space between
Scrub pine and fir directed our climb:
No past marks of others seen
Now marked this our time.

There, there in this sub-freezing, gale-driven noon
We found a shrew foraging for small mites.
She was unconcerned by this place, this site of winter's force.
She plunged in and out of drifting snows;
She sought the edges of birch and fir
To dive deep into the white cover and re-surface,
Not even gasping for air.

We broke tree line. No hope lay
In the solid white of the storm's worth;
Between cairns only blindness to essay.
Here was for us the season's dearth.

And the shrew with the will to strive
Without a thought or concern:
Will she thus survive?
And will I remember the stern
Will, the shrew's plight

As I descend the trail's turn?
Or succumb unto death's fright?

Geese

I hear them again: the voices.
It is the second time this week—
there is a low overcast—a bar
against my sight, but
they're there as assuredly as I am here.

Neighbors, who abhor the snow and ice,
ask why I stay; why not
follow the voices; I would rather
head north into winter's face
And I try to tell them so.

I believe I understand their search,
their want for warmth; but
can they know my want? a want
for seasons and for weather?
The calm these voices seek, I'll forgo

this year as I have year after year …
The wood is stacked, seasoned; the woolens
unpacked and aired; the storm windows hung;
and I am ready with slippers, to read, to sit
with you, my Love, warmed within winter's wrath.

A Brown Creeper & the Snake
                              -Warwick, Mass.

The snow packed trail gradually descends
through pine stands
and ancient oaks and
   crosses
a curb-formed bridge
of pasture stones,
ascends and bends
toward the north.

Others have passed here though it seems not so today...
snake-like it enters
The Enchanted Forest
of tall, slim, and red-skinned pines.

There are occasional crossings
where local residents
follow water courses
          and glacier formed ridges ...

I have not sauntered here before;
though something about the passing
is familiar;
   nothing is the same, yet
it is ....

Near the trail's terminus
          pinned to a pine
a warning:
'Snake Crossing'. designed
like Tlingit art ...
of a snake curled, a Uroboros ...

I am ready to follow
my return where through the leafless woods
I see the cliffs of Mt. Grace ...

I know I cannot stay my visit
to listen and watch
a Brown Creeper
drift
like an autumn leaf
to a pine's base and to crawl
up toward heaven ...

I will while away for awhile
timeless joy ...

But
winter's cold creeps into my fingers
and through the leather
of my stationary boots ...
        and a voice calls as if
to remind me of my place ...

Before I turn to retrace
my tracks back, to depart
      this day's enchantment,
I with a whisper-like sssh, sssh, ... sssh*
listen for the Creeper's soft, clear call;
for he speaks, in his solitude,
of companionship;
he floats descending
to again rise with his incessant, upward
zigzagged search
        for sustenance ...

          as now
I too ... I too ...

———

*repetitive

Late November

Where the fields are mowed
dandelions—a scattered few
—flower

In this month of frosts
       & thoughts of tombs
       their hardiness
forms miniature suns
with innumerable rays
in hay-tinted skies:

dwarfed designs of spring.

For them, as with me,
the season is too advanced
for simple summer fruition.

We, in a May-like mood
stay the day
with these late blooms
of visible gold
       & invisible tints
in the sharp, pure,
limited light of autumn.

I hear voices—distant
       and ancient—
singing of fool-hearted glory
       of second youth …

Warning, oh yes, warning …

Such cynicisms
       be not our guides …
 on our lyres
we celebrate this second spring.

Edward Hopper

I am the man standing at the window.
The city before me a desert of peeling paint
and blank walls. Squares and rectangles;
no curves: for I am not the naked woman
standing near the bed; though we are nearly
the same in our rooms—alone, staring, knowing

what lies before us is as dreary as the blank
scene outside our windows and inside
our undecorated rooms. With the gray sky,
the gray walls, the gray unoccupied streets
and the gray of this room I cannot remember
if its before dawn or after dusk that

I stare into. She, who I am not, stands
before her bed that's neither turned back nor wrinkled;
for her it is dawn; she has been out all night
and now tries to imagine sleeping at night
in this dark in this bed in this room, she's forgotten
where she spent the night, she is not rested

and not hungry. Who are we; the two of us
so motionless, subjects before our objects:
my vacant city; her unslept in, smooth bed.
What carried us here today to our
private places? and will carry us out of
our shadowless rooms into some gray future ...?

For my Senior who had a Stroke

Your left side lost refuses your will to obey;
It drags along like an impish limp child
Appended as to its mother's hand and way.

I found you in the stairwell alone today
Grasping the rail and straining to be wild
But your left side lost refuses your will to obey;

You carried the crippled self with masked dismay
To refuse my aid for your will was not reconciled
To be held as to a mother's hand and way.

You, the charitable, now for a gift pray:
Not the masked sign of mending that reviled
Your left side who refused your will to obey.

It is the hopelessness of decay
That leadens your young heart to be exiled
From being your mother's hand and way;

And makes this our fear of the night, of day
Where the good receives losses compiled:
Your left side lost refuses your will to obey,
Limp without your mother's hand and way.

Four Gifts

1. A Feather

There is a song here
I search for—a rising up the chromatic scale;
it summoned
me into this area of slash,
separated me from a clear path.
I stand in the puckerbrush of clear cutting
motionless, listening...
I see the horizon hills
in four directions. I've been called to this center.
Around me are the songs
and motions
of all the living, of water,
and of stone.
The chromatic song is repeated again and again
in this pathless
overgrowth, this area of slash:

2. An Antler

On my descent from the height that commands
this region, these woods, and this lake,
I left the trail holding the declining sun at my back,
following my shadow home.
Above me a lone whistle,
the call of a hawk; then the soft, nearly soundless, motion of air
lowered a primary of the Broad-Winged.
I placed this amulet in my hat
as I continued into timber trash disguised
under the spreading raspberries.
                        I twisted through a beech grove
onto an animal path back into the berries where
like a lumbered limb lay a moose antler. And it spoke:
take me home for I am a gift of the world's interlacings.
Seven years later
a Gray Squirrel's gnaws blunt
the antler's spars.

3. A cleat

In the evening
I paddle along the shore westward; the large lake
nearly calm mirrors the sky's convex lid.
A trout rises along side my canoe.
A kingfisher rattles.
A red-orange waterscape lightens my motion.
A pair of loons call.
These impulses invite inclusion. Near shore
swallows skim the surface
where I find a floating end of a piece of hemp.
I can see where it disappears into the lake's darkness.
Hand over hand I lift it as if it were an anchor;
on the dark's end is a cleat
from a wharf, a way to secure my self
to this depth.

4. Dri-ki.

Darkness, when so near
to the summer solstice crawls,
as slowly as a painted turtle
letting me drift gently back to my woodland cabin.
Near the shore a piece of dri-ki unlike any other floats:
it is designed as is Einstein's four dimensional world:
a collage carved into the root's shape.
A soft voice—perhaps the voice of the thrush—
sings: "Take it. It is for your wife, a reminder
of the female, the center of an ever changing
universe, ever alive.
Present it to her for she, the artist, holds
the power of sympathy, the tolerance
of need, the knowledge
of all our relatives."

A Mountain Hike

I set out with my trekking poles & a light pack:
a wind breaker, an apple, nuts and fruits, and chocolate.

The trail crosses a dry brook, passes through beech,
Yellow Birch, and climbs across granite outcroppings.

How far my legs will hold out is a guess.
Though the ravens have not flown south I wish

for the companionship of a Gray Jay. I have
some nuts and seeds if he gently glides near me.

A Winter Wren surprises me with a song
and an Oven Bird skiddles along the forest floor.

This is far enough just above tree line. It's clear
to the south mountains, the western hills

and in the north to the wide river. My descent
recalls scenes that erase the worries of age …

Lily Keep

Weep, weep, I weep for my climb is steep,
Covered with thorns sharp; my way's upon a scarp
Of loose talus where I can no longer climb or creep:

You, my confidant, my love, gone, done: two decades
Destroyed by my declared task, my want to unmask;
And our light, our past into present darkness fades.

I alone, ill, weep for my fate, set in a web with no thread,
In a maze with no escape. No clew, no wings, no shape
Waits to guide me: the minotaur will another maiden be fed.

I crossed your calm boundary, your pleasures uncommitted
Though gentle, soft, kind; and I was gladly blind
In innocent, pained hope desiring the unpermitted
Where no intimacy could struggle to a view unfettered

A Crossing

I saw it crossing the street.
It limped and dragged its feet
tacking slightly sideways; its back
humped; it was black, all black …

My cat missing, since the day before, surely
has white toes and a white spot on his belly—
These should have his identity sealed,
but could they not have been concealed?

Now inert by the road it lies
—an amorphous mass of fur,
a black mesh bag—& dies.
I, in unsuitable fear, cannot stir.

The Bangor & Aroostook RR
A Parable for Franz Kafka

The train is in the station
As always almost I am
in my seat already—early—
I am not sure where I am destined

The train, I know, is slow
and its departure early—
before 5 AM. It will travel a
short distance for an extension

of time—I hear someone on the platform
explain It is the Milk Train.
And I know already it will stop
at many, many farms for coffee

and sour milk doughnuts—naturally
deep fried—and oh ever so delicious
if not sweet—it takes time
to again get up enough steam—

Someone on the platform cries—
jacketed men joke — laugh grimacingly—
where are their families going
—I do not know this either

We move—buckle—and bang
to a stop. The watchers cheer—
I am not sure if mockingly
or almost perhaps envyingly

We should already be there by sunset
on a wharf by an inland sea—or
if not there certainly almost somewhere—
It matters little—handkerchiefs flutter—

Red-bellied Cooter

She lay on the road
her plates
haphazardly smashed, caved in;
she lay not in the red of her belly
but of the blood that oozed
after the boys
stained their aluminum bats
on her back ...

I thought of where she came from
... the land of cattails
on the east side of the tarmac
and where she was heading
... perhaps home,
on the drier side of the road;

... and of the farm boys
who leapt off
their rusty red
and silver bikes
coming home from a loss;
and of the raising
of their spirits
as they swung
and struck her successfully ...
yes, finally got some hits
to help their averages.

Now they could come home
with pleasure,
enjoyment on their faces
and in their strides
... not the hang-dog pose
that the game's loss
proffered them.

They must have laughed
and shouted as they each
took a swing in a motion
not as when at bat
but as with an axe
splitting ash and oak,
but she did not split,
divide cleanly along
growth lines
as does hardwood, but just
caved in ... caved in ... and yet
the pleasure was greater
... not ruined by an assigned chore.
This was for them
victory ... at last.

Mt. Grace

I left the trail
today
to go where none had turned seared leaves;

I listened for the Ravens' words,
for the Redtails' screams;

I write not
of deer trails or natural paths heralded by wilderness walkers ...
though others tell me
of puckerbrush pain
and muddy depressions of unkempt walks...

At the first incline
I pass
a layered rock and higher up
a stone wall's gap. I climb

the pitch to where it slackens into a platform ...
to a man-curbed pool
where no trail's remains inform ...
where a nervous, darting Winter Wren slips under a fallen pine ...
beyond the paths ...
I keep an eye
on the sky
to find
a height of land ... covered with grass from a field
now claimed by second growth.

I sit upon this incidental peak of Grace
for today I will not will
to go further ...

The view's through trees ...
toward blue:
a ridge of seamless waves ...

Seasons in the Mind

Seasonal [Autumn]

In the field lies dormant
my garden marked by three
nights of rime. Tomatoes,
squash, basil, and cucumbers
sag saddened. An old rusty
fork with one missing tine
and chicken wire set to host
vines seem as stranded
in the dawn's river fog as
aging grandparents—the
harvest of a quiet and a
season-weathered friendship.

Seasonal [Winter]

In the field lies dormant
my garden marked by a fork
for turning soil; the winter
snows shrink; the fork grows—
again the garden will be tuned
by hand like a fine parlor grand
in anticipation of spread seeds—
the issue of a quiet, dormant,
snow-weathered friendship.

Seasonal [Spring]

In the field lies my garden
marked by melting.
Spring is on the wind;
The snows have receded
revealing autumn's mulch.
I clear the covering, fork the soil,
spread the seeds of squash,
basil, and cucumbers on raised
rows inside the rusted chicken wire.
I plant what will be, with
tender care, fall's pleasures:
season-weathered friends.

Seasonal [Summer]

In the field my garden lies
not dormant. My stained fork
pitched into the rich soil
marks the east side. In the center
an hermaphroditic scarecrow
guards beans, squash, tomatoes,
and lettuces. The rusted chicken
wire supports cucumbers
and morning glories. Wrens,
phoebes, and kingbirds
harvest insects from the vines.
Pleasant odors of brushed herbs
— basil, oregano, parsley, and dill —
remind me of cooking together,
of our seasoned friendship.

The Sparrow Hawk,
-Revisited after Forty Years

He is not a watcher of our ways:
neither of our regional routes
nor of our inner maze.

What are our swirlings to him
And his to us: seasonal
arrivals and departures?
He finds a denuded branch or
roadside wires to alight upon
and at times he hangs still in air
while we travel in our times
and places foul and fair
viewing each to each.

Now when I shade my view
to see him against the sun
on a day of cloudless blue
I no longer have a foolish whim
that his incessant zigzag
makes him a king and I vassal;
and my once loneliness
evaporates as the sun
forgives the morning mist,

and thus our maps intersect
in neither fear nor respect
as he rises on the noontime
and I know that what he does,
he does and what I do, I do.

Kinsman Poems

Arrival

A rooster—
A silhouette of Mt. Kinsman—
the rest sleep

It is clearing ...
         an unknown bird sings.

The depression in the mowed yard
is where a driveway
to the barn once lay—
   like the farmer, the farm, and the struggle
   with the land and season—
it is a trace
masked by new inhabitants ...
the history remains in the air,
in the land
by the restored farmhouse
where guests
sit on the narrow porch rocking,
rocking with generations of worn boards and torn lives.

Sunrise: mountain shadows retreat...

I. Dawn Under Kinsman Ridge, 8/4/13

This land, not yet home—it's incredible.
The ordinary—goldenrod, berries edible,

a Solitary Vireo in the valley, and voices
of the distant mountain cataracts—has

a clarity unknown in the bustle of suburban woe.
Time suspended grants creation's ebb and flow.

    * * * *

Again—in August—I sit on the narrow porch
of Freeland Acres; the clouds, a light gray pilch,

hang on the shoulders of Kinsman, sun-tinged
they drift southward; windows of blue are fringed

white … And in the morning stillness I heard
a swirling whirl—by my ear a hummingbird.

I slowly notice dark-enigma's inner patterns:
The emptiness from which rise all illusions …

[the lines in italics are from The Mountain Poems of Meng Hao-jan
as translated by David Hinton]

Mountain Air

The mountain
in clear air wears
a stocking cap,
I heard it said,
    as if
      it were
        in a long winter sleep.

Another voice with majestic authority
knows that that's not so
and assures us that it appears merely
as an active volcano;

with the sun's rising
      the realist sees
that the hat
is nothing just
morning mountain clouds
that dissipate
to make the mountain
          sublime.

And—like morning moods—
to again become
a cloud-shrouded sculpture.

Plums

My legs ache; to seek relief
I read about plums in February
by two spirited poets
separated by a thousand years:
one Chinese, one American;
one male, one female —

Their white blossoms like a spring snow
warm my heart—
One watches young maidens
gathering petals
the other walks in rain.

I sit and read; I know their words'
warmth
for it infiltrates my pain

I lie in August in cool mountain air
to sleep time's last hours
under his pine tree decorated comforter.
   * * *

its joys, its power to release,
to awaken
the inchoate power of sleep.

[the poets: Meng Hao-jan (689-740);
Emily Warn (Contemporary)]

Under the Mountain

In the afternoon, after we've slept,
the neighbor's cock crows;
we find a thin overcast kept
on the mountain
where a crest
beckons
and we know to leave pluck
to younger spirits;
to accept our luck
and remember why we rest.

11. Mt. Kinsman, Dusk

I keep emptiness whole
rocking on the narrow, slanted porch
with my feet on the white rail.

I peer at the great mountain.

The sun will soon send one last ray
upon Kinsman's north peak …

we are brothers—not twins—
slowly expanding & shrinking …
in the fading light …

last summer's constellations rise …

Easton, N.H.

I live up the road from where the poet lives;
my fields are as hard to till
as the rhythmic rows of words he finds.

We, both, when tired, are like kinsmen
who sit on narrow farmhouse porches
watching the weather's power darken

the mountain's chin, ragged brow, and marred body—
when light fades we weigh

the awful dominance of its outline

against a starlit sky ... a horizon where
soon a partial moon rises and throws
behind us on white walls our shadows.

Reflection

When home again I will travel
this journal
to discover the sights, the sounds
that abound
within its leaves and, as with a good walk,
carefully stalk
its senses to know what was
there before
as with jazz's
improvisational core

Acknowledgements

"You're a Poem" was published in *Mobius*, Methuen, MA

"The Red Maple" and "Thursday to Thursday" were published in the *Westbere Review*, Tulsa, OK.

"Black Nebula" was published in *The Greenfield Review*, Greenfield Center NY

"Dewey Avenue", "Voices", "Sleepwalkers", and "For my Senior who had a Stroke" were published in *Equinox*, Shelburne Falls, MA

The line "If you leave your simple door frame" in my poem "The Open Door Frame" (Page 55) is the first line from Candice Stover's poem "Surroundings" in her collection *Holding Patterns*. The line is used with her permission.

There are numerous folks that have been supportive of my writing. Especially Margot, my partner, who has been most helpful with her criticism and suggestions. I am grateful to Mike, my son, for his keen eye and gentleness, who proof read this manuscript and made suggestions for changes in the poems. Ann Gengarelly, Bob Tucker, Baron Wormser, Frank Olson, and Marguerite Lenz are among those who have helped me. And I want to thank Paul Richmond, who has encouraged me to read my poems and is most supportive as my editor and publisher.

www.ingramcontent.com/pod-product-compliance
Lightning Source LLC
Chambersburg PA
CBHW071158090426
42736CB00012B/2373